MOTHER!

IT'S ALL IN THE ATTITUDE

2010

To Jen,
Always keep your
fantastic sense of humor.
It will serve you well.
Love always,
Noël and Ed

P.S. Michael: Chapter Four

SELLERS
PUBLISHING

Published by Sellers Publishing, Inc.
Copyright © 2009 Sellers Publishing, Inc.

Artwork © 2009 PostMark Press
All rights reserved.

Edited by: Mark Chimsky-Lustig & Robin Haywood
Book Design: George Corsillo, Design Monsters
Production Layouts: Charlotte Smith

Sellers Publishing, Inc.
P.O. Box 818, Portland, Maine 04104
For ordering information:
(800) 625-3386 toll free
Visit our Web site: www.sellerspublishing.com • E-mail: rsp@rsvp.com

ISBN: 13: 978-1-4162-0543-2

10 9 8 7 6 5 4 3 2 1

Printed and bound in China.

MOTHER!

IT'S ALL IN THE ATTITUDE

A Guide to
Surviving Motherhood

Kathy Alpert

Dedication

To my mother Sylvia Green — and all mothers everywhere.
— *Kathy Alpert*

"God could not be everywhere, so She created mothers."
— *ancient proverb with a twist*

Preface

Hi gals.

Are you worried that you're about to trade your diva days for changing Pampers and taste-testing strained prunes? Or, on the other end of the spectrum, have you been in the mommy trenches so long that even your husband refers to you as "Mom"? Buck up, salvation is here! Whether you've just found out you're going to be a new mother or you've reached that stage of motherhood where you need a "refresher course" on how to fortify yourself for the journey — this book reveals how to make the most of being a mom without sacrificing your own unique and fabulous self. In *Mother! It's All in the Attitude*, you'll be introduced to a wide array of moms who simply refuse to take their role too seriously. Follow their example and you'll be set for life!

As Maria Callas once said, "Everyone should have a look"— an outward style that reflects their inner personality. Think of Donna

Reed vacuuming in pearls or a very pregnant Angelina Jolie wearing her "Breakfast at Tiffany's" Chanel sunglasses. As a practicing mother, you may not always have time to achieve your look, but you do always have time to cultivate attitude! A knowing nod and a quip can do wonders for putting everything in its proper perspective and helping you to maintain your sanity. Are your kids driving you crazy? Just count the days until you ship them off to college. Have you been enlisted to whip up a platter of chocolate chip cookies for Junior's bakesale? Just hand Junior the mixer and tell him to have fun. Even when you begin to feel overwhelmed, there is a way to see the glass as being half full (and let's hope it contains a yummy martini, shaken not stirred).

The mothers in this book will show you how to cook, clean, go off to work, and raise the kids while keeping a distinctly devil-may-care outlook and shooting a few well-placed zingers. Remember, it's all in the attitude!

Contents

Mother!

CHAPTER 1

(or Add an "S" and It's "Smother")

Stat:

The average mother in the U.S. spends 5,472 hours carpooling her children.

Solution:

Leather upholstered seat equipped with warmer and massager!

Look girls, I'll wear the same hat as you but I just might add a little something extra to *my* milk!

I woke up and smelled the coffee. And once I added a little Bailey's it tasted just fine.

Stat:

The typical mom says "No!" an average of 145 times a week.

Solution: Next time your kids ask you for anything, just say the three little words that will save your sanity: "Ask your father."

Okay, kids, you can't scare me.
I'm a MOTHER!
And I know how to disconnect
your Internet service!

I'm on the phone with the
Lost Children's Fund and
if you girls don't behave,
guess who they're getting
as a donation?

18

Attitude Advice:

A lot of problems can be resolved by spending the day in bed. If you're lucky, the husband and kids won't starve before they find the refrigerator.

22

Quandary:

I drop my kids off wherever they want to go, but somehow they always manage to find their way home.

There's nothing like the
first day of summer camp!

25

Attitude Advice:
Cocktail or nap?
Remember, your kids
are depending on you.
Opt for the cocktail.

26

28

29

30

Stat:

More than 75% of
families experience
stress during vacation.

Solution:

At the start of your trip,
take your kids to the
biggest attraction you
can find (at Dollywood,
drop them off at the
Thunderhead Roller
Coaster).

Pick them up when
you're ready to leave
the state.

If it was only this easy
to train the kids.
And the husband.

32

33

ith Mama   CHAPTER 2

My Favorite Frozen Foods?

Frozen Margarita
Frozen Daiquiri
Frozen Mai Tai

37

Desperate housewife
or domestic goddess?
You decide.

39

40

See how clever I am?
I'll serve it all with
bowls of ketchup —
it kills the taste and is
practically a vegetable.

41

The 7 Stages of Kitchen Fatigue

1. Denial – A feeling of numbness while making a roast.

2. Guilt – Disbelief is replaced by unbelievable pain (often experienced while using Hamburger Helper).

3. Anger and Bargaining – Your random acts of lashing out (asking "Why me?") are followed by bargaining ("I'll go without 'Desperate Housewives' for a month – just get me out of this @#%# kitchen!")

4. Depression – You let yourself go to pot, recklessly running the blender at unsafe speeds.

5. The "Turning Point" – The sight of boxes of Shake and Bake no longer plunge you into a pit of despair.

6. Working Through – You become more functional and can even look at the stove without thinking of Sylvia Plath.

7. Acceptance and Hope – Like millions of other moms, you find the inner strength to cope!

44

What was I thinking?

Note to self:

- Remember, I'm not Becky Homecky.

- Next time offer huge financial incentive for a batch of homemade cookies.

- Burn *Betty Crocker* cookbook.

Baking doesn't make
me deliriously happy
. . . just delirious!

46

I find the best way to add zing to my
48 fruitcake is by putting in extra fruit and
nuts with a scotch on the side.

49

I try to be a good example, but I usually end up being a dire warning instead.

52

I like my meat rare and
my plastic strong.   53

I dreamt of an alternative universe of non-stop dinner parties . . . time for rehab?

56

57

(M!)

Just a coincidence?

Stat #1:

The average mom goes grocery shopping 156 times a year.

Stat #2:

The average mom loses 3,698 brain cells before she turns fifty.

60

Know what I'm making
for dinner tonight?
Reservations.

61

Domestic Diva

CHAPTER 3

(or I Live to Clean! Not!)

64

There's no household chore
that a little chardonnay
doesn't make easier.

I'm saving the planet by not cleaning — the layers of dirt and grime on my windows help filter harmful rays from entering the house.

67

68

My idea of exercise is running the washing machine.

Attitude Advice:

Every once in a while
even domestic divas need
to take a break.

70

I've always dreamed of being stacked . . . but not quite this way!

73

74

Attitude Advice:

How do I keep up with the cooking, cleaning, shopping and still manage to keep this cute apron spotless? I outsource.

Out of the frying pan
and into the vodka!

77

78

*Laundry this clean
should never go on the kids.*

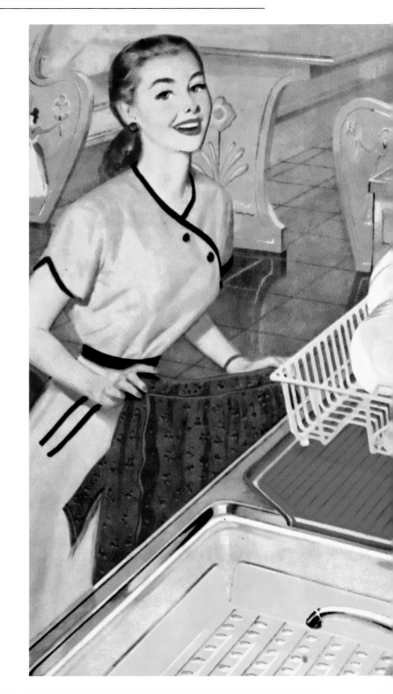

Stat:

A typical mom washes
dishes 82,125 times over
the course of her life.

Solution:

Get a wife!

82

No thanks, I'll wait till the
riding version comes out.

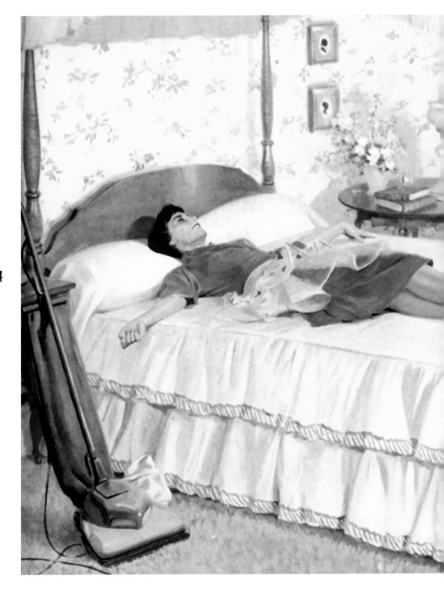

They say housecleaning never killed anyone, but why risk it?

Accessorize!

CHAPTER 4

(or Every Good Mother Deserves Diamonds)

88

They just raised my credit limit!

89

I . . . want . . . my . . . Manolos!

90

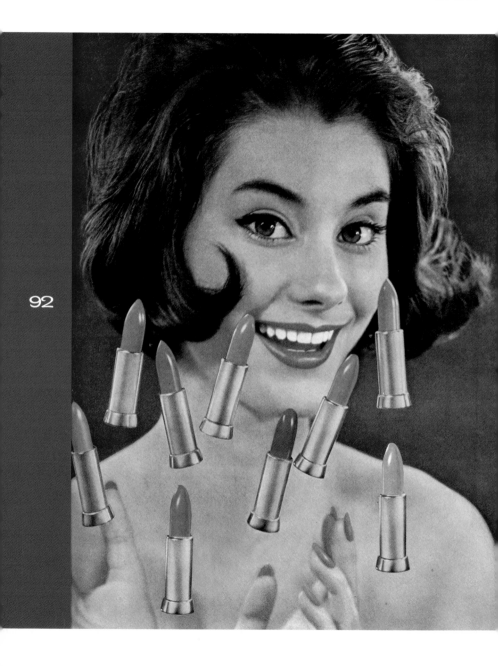

92

So many colors to choose from
. . . so little time!

94

I believe in girth control.

Attitude Advice:

What to say when your husband buys you a cubic zirconia ring instead of that two-carat diamond at Tiffany's:

"Oh, you shouldn't have Dave ... You really, really shouldn't have."

98

When I commune with nature,
I prefer my gems to be exotic:

Alaskan Diamond

Cornflower Sapphire

Rocky Mountain Ruby

Zambian Emerald

100

I feel like I'm wearing
a barrette on steroids.

(M!)

Stat:

The average mom sacrifices for her kids, forgoing purchases for themselves 95% of the time.

Solution:

Make that 5% really memorable!

103

I've done my part
to jumpstart the economy.

Yes sir! I make motherhood look good.

I Want It All!

CHAPTER 5

(Kiss Donna Reed and Harriet Nelson Goodbye)

110

We're celebrating the $300,000 that our investment club made this year!

112

I may have earned
my MBA at an
Ivy League school but
wearing pink makes me
feel positively giddy.

114

We have a "modern" relationship — he watches the kids and I'm a senior v.p. at a multinational corporation!

Bedroom or boardroom?
I'm weighing and
considering all options.

117

In this family I
bring home the bacon
~ and cook it too!

119

I've traded Dr. Spock
for Suze Orman!

I Want It All!

I don't need a map . . .
I know where I'm going.

123

Who says I can't balance work and family? I'm teaching my daughter how to break the glass ceiling as I drive her to pre-K!

125

Motherhood.
It's all in the attitude.

127